THEORY WHY

In Which the Boss Solves the Riddle of Quality

JOHN GUASPARI

amacom
American Management Association

Library of Congress Cataloging-in-Publication Data

Guaspari, John.
    Theory why.

    1. Quality of products—Miscellanea. I. Title.
HD38.G767   1986   658.5′62   86-47593
ISBN 0-8144-5876-9

Printing number

10 9 8 7 6 5 4 3 2

For
Michael

Prologue

Once upon a time there was a company called Punctuation Inc.

It was a company which was spectacularly successful commercially, breathtakingly innovative technologically, admirably responsible civicly, and—most important of all—terribly necessary grammatically.

Because Punctuation Inc. made, as you've probably guessed by now, punctuation marks.

Periods, commas, question marks.
Semicolons, colons, exclamation points.
Brackets and parentheses.
Dashes and ellipses.
Hyphens and apostrophes.
Quotation marks, closed and open.

You name it, they made it.

What's more, if they made it, you probably bought it.

Because ever since Rufus Punctum, Punctuation Inc.'s founder, discovered the first punctuation mark (as it happens, a question mark—but that's another story) and started up the business—the industry!—the company had been the runaway market leader.

Over the years, more people used punctuation marks from Punctuation Inc. for more different applications than all the competitor's products combined:

> For written English, such as, for example, the page you're reading now.
>
> For spoken English, such as, for example, the question mark you used when you asked the storekeeper if she had this book in stock.
>
> For the heart-tugging plaintiveness of the baby's cry.
>
> For the rigor and precision of the scientist's formulation.
>
> For the rhythm and timing of the comic's one-liner.
>
> For the crystalline resonance of the poet's art.
>
> For the nation-binding power of the stateman's speech.
>
> For the homely utilitarianism of the grocery list.

For all these uses and many, many more, Punctuation Inc. had been, until recently, the runaway market leader.

Which brings us to our story.

Because recently, a company called Process Inc. had been outperforming Punctuation Inc. in a number of rather important categories.

Like productivity.

And profitability.

And market share.

Yes. Customers were switching their allegiance from Punctuation Inc. to Process Inc., and that fact had caused a good number of the good people at Punctuation Inc. to spend a good deal of their time asking themselves a very basic (and very good) question.

Why?

That, in fact, is the very question that was troubling The Boss very late on this particular night (actually, very early on this particular morning) as he sat brooding in his office at Punctuation Inc.'s corporate headquarters.

Oh, he knew that those customers—those ex-customers, to be exact—had *said* that their reason for switching over to Process Inc. was Quality, since it was his own market research efforts that had uncovered that fact.

He knew that Punctuation Inc. had undertaken an unprecedentedly massive campaign to address those Quality problems, since he had, after all, personally directed that campaign.

And he knew that they had appeared to be making progress in those efforts, since he had the internal Quality reports to "prove" it.

But he also knew that just eight hours earlier a disgruntled customer—a disgruntled ex-customer, to be exact—had poured out (metaphorically) a list of complaints about the Quality of Punctuation Inc. products in The Boss's office, and then poured out (literally) the contents of a large, brown sack full of the offending products onto The Boss's desk.

● ● ●

Periods.
Semicolons.
Question marks.
Ellipses.
Dashes.
Parentheses.
Brackets.
Apostrophes.
Asterisks.

All in a dusty black heap.

The Boss knew all this as he sifted his fingers through the dusty black heap that still covered his desk.

We've researched and analyzed our

Quality problems to death, he thought to himself. We've made some progress, but we don't seem to be able to come up with the definitive answer. Why?

We've taken dramatic, decisive actions. But they don't seem to give us the desired results. Why?

We care a great, great deal, and yet that caring does not seem to translate into effective solutions. Why?

Looking across the room at the portrait of his company's founder and his predecessor (several administrations removed), he softly uttered the question aloud: "Why, Rufus, why?"

Absent-mindedly, he scratched the letters W H Y on a pad on his desk. That, thought The Boss, seeing what he had written, is a serious question. It calls for a serious punctuation mark.

He opened a desk drawer and sorted through his supplies tray until he found what he was looking for: an Industrial Grade question mark. He affixed it to the legend on his desk so that it now read:

He stared at that question and thought about it for a long, long time. And the longer he stared and thought, the more angry and frustrated he became.

Until, all at once, The Boss's anger got the best of him. He swept his arm across the desk, scattering the entire dusty black heap across the room.

The entire dusty black heap, that is, except for a single exclamation point that was left on his desk, directly in front of him.

The Boss cocked his wrist to flick it, too, onto the floor. But his wrist locked as he saw what lay on his desk.

"I know a Quality solution when I see it," exclaimed The Boss. "And finally, *finally*, I see it!"

"Why?" he asked himself, challengingly "Exactly. *Why!*" he answered, triumphantly.

This is the story of what he finally saw.

ood morning!" said The Boss to his right-hand man and his left-hand man as they entered his office. "And how are you gentlemen on this fine, fine morning?"

"Fine," said the right-hand man.

"Fine," said the left-hand man.

"And you?" they asked, in unison.

"Couldn't be better!" The Boss responded enthusiastically. Motioning them to be seated at the conference table across the room, he added matter-of-factly (for dramatic effect), "After all, I think I've finally discovered the secret to solving our Quality problems."

The right-hand man and left-hand man looked at each other in silence as they took their seats.

On the one hand, the right-hand man's thoughts turned to the various other "solutions" to Punctuation Inc.'s Quality problems that The Boss had discovered in the past. And—no disrespect intended—hadn't they turned out to be illusory?

On the other hand, the left-hand man's thoughts turned to The Boss that they had left the night before. Despondent. Brooding over the dusty black heap poured out by the complaining customer. Not a hint of this morning's ebullience.

But both the right-hand man and the left-hand man had lived through all the months of false starts and frustration—the right-hand man running the Quality program in the engineering department, the left-hand man running the Quality program in the manufacturing department—and they had come through it with a deep and abiding respect for The Boss. When he spoke with such conviction, that was reason enough to be excited.

And it was with just such conviction that The Boss pressed on. "I have decided on a course of action which, I'm confident, will result in a reaffirmation of Punctuation Inc. as the clear-cut number one company in the punctuation mark business," he said.

The right-hand man and the left-hand man leaned forward in anticipation. Just maybe it really *would* be different this time!

"You two," continued The Boss, in a slightly hushed, slightly conspiratorial tone, "have a very key role to play."

Their anticipation grew keener.

"In fact," added The Boss, "that role begins right now."

The right-hand man and left-hand man could barely contain their excitement.

"Yes! Of course!" said the right-hand man.

"What would you like us to do?" asked the left-hand man.

The Boss smiled and nodded, reassured. "I knew I could count on you. What I'd like you two to do is . . ."

The right-hand man and left-hand man leaned forward in the keenest anticipation yet.

"Relinquish your responsibilities for Quality in the manufacturing and engineering departments."

The right-hand man and left-hand man were stunned.

"*That's* the important role you want us to play?" asked left-hand man.

"To *stop* being responsible for Quality in those departments?" asked the right-hand man.

"Yes, that's right," said The Boss. Then, noticing their crestfallen looks, he added, "Is something the matter?"

"Well," began the left-hand man, "it's just that we think you're overreacting a little, that's all."

"Yes," said the right-hand man. "We know that that customer had some complaints last night about the Quality of our products, maybe even some legitimate complaints. But is that reason enough to take us off the job?"

"Do you really think—" the right-hand man began.

"—that blaming us will solve the Quality problems?" the left-hand man concluded.

"Blame you?" asked The Boss in astonishment. "I wouldn't think of blaming you! I blame myself for what happened last night!"

They looked puzzled. The Boss noticed.

"Let me explain," he said. "Late last night—actually, early this morning—I realized that we've been coming at our Quality problems the wrong way. *I've* been coming at our Quality problems the wrong way.

"We sit over here in corporate headquarters, and we think we're doing pretty well with some of the pieces of Quality, such as manufacturing," he said, turning toward the left-hand man, "or engineering," he added, with a nod toward the right-hand man.

"But from a customer's point of view—an *ex*-customer's point of view—there's no such thing as 'pieces of Quality.' You've either got total Quality, or you've got no Quality at all.

"Total Quality is a matter for the total organization, not just for manufacturing and engineering—the two most obvious places to turn.

"And total Quality can't be run as a 'corporate program.' It requires total ownership by the people on the line!"

The right-hand man and left-hand man thought they were beginning to understand.

"So you've decided that the way to

solve our Quality problem is to give responsibility for Quality directly to the people on
the line?" said the right-hand man.

"That's right," said The Boss.

"And you're going to expand our Quality efforts to all departments, beyond just
manufacturing and engineering?" said the
left-hand man.

"Correct," said The Boss.

"And as a result of that," said the left-
hand man, "we'll see a solution to our Quality
problem?"

"Once and for all?" added the right-hand
man.

The Boss stopped them in their tracks.

"Oh, no," he said. "Frankly, I don't think it
has a chance."

"You don't really think it has a chance—"
the right-hand man began.

"And yet you're going to do it anyway?"
the left-hand man concluded.

"That's right," said The Boss.

They looked at each other in disbelief.

"We have just one more question," they
stated in unison.

"Which is?" replied The Boss.

"*Why?*" they asked.

"Exactly!" exclaimed The Boss. "You *do*
understand!"

What had been simple disbelief now
spilled over into total bewilderment. But
their instincts took over (you don't get to be a
right-hand man or a left-hand man by playing the fool) and they decided to accept The

Boss's praise without comment. They listened silently as The Boss outlined his plan.

Three months had passed since The Boss had outlined his plan to his right-hand man and left-hand man, and he knew that this week's staff meeting, scheduled to begin in just a few moments, was crucial to that plan's success.

The Manufacturing Manager was the first to arrive for the staff meeting.

"Welcome," welcomed The Boss. "As usual, the first to arrive!"

The Manufacturing Manager nodded a quick hello, hurried to his customary seat at the opposite end of the table from The Boss, and allowed himself to relax by sitting forward on the edge of his chair, rhythmically chewing gum, tapping a pencil on the water glass in front of him, and pumping his right heel off the floor.

The right-hand man and left-hand man were the next to arrive. Greetings were exchanged as they took their places at (could it have been any other way?) The Boss's right hand and left hand, respectively.

The Finance Manager entered the room. "Is this meeting a freebie," he asked, "or can I charge my time back to you?"

"Handle it any way you like," replied The Boss, by now both used to and bemused by the Finance Manager's "creative" approach to time management. "I trust your judgment to do what's right."

"Thank you," said the Finance Manager, taking a seat to the left of the Manufacturing Manager. He was grateful for The Boss's trust and made a mental note not to bill The Boss for the time it had taken for him to walk from his office to The Boss's.

The next to arrive was the Engineering Manager. "I trust I'm not late," she said. "According to my chronometer, the meeting isn't scheduled to begin for another two-point-three-seven minutes."

"Why don't we get started?" asked the Manufacturing Manager, picking up the pace of his tapping and pumping.

"We can start," said The Boss, "as soon as the others arrive. After all, we still have—"

"Exactly zero-point-five-six minutes," stated the Engineering Manager.

No sooner had she said this than the last two members of The Boss's staff—the Marketing Manager and the Human Resources Manager—entered the room.

"I would have been here a little earlier," explained the Human Resources Manager as he pulled up a chair to the left of the left-hand man, "but I had to share with someone over the phone."

"Did we go to party lines for the phone system?" asked the Manufacturing Manager.

"I think he meant that he had to 'talk to' someone on the phone," answered the Engineering Manager.

The Finance Manager was intrigued. "Wouldn't party lines be a lot cheaper?" he asked.

The Manufacturing Manager's impatience was increasing, as evidenced by the heightened sloshing of the water glasses along the table in tempo with his heel pumping.

"I would just like to announce," announced the Marketing Manager as she took the last remaining seat at the table, directly to the right of the Manufacturing Manager, "that I've just done a study which reveals that more water is being sloshed out of my drinking glass than out of all the other drinking glasses combined!"

"That and precisely zero-point-one dollar will get you a cup of coffee," added the Engineering Manager, throwing in her zero-point-zero-two dollar's worth.

"Are they running a special on coffee in the cafeteria?" asked the Finance Manager, starting to rise.

"Please, please. Sit down. Coffee is being brought in," said The Boss. "I think we should begin. And really, my agenda is very simple. I just have one question for each of you. It's been three months since we began our expanded Quality efforts in all operating units. How are your departments doing?"

"I can answer that," said the Manufacturing Manager, picking up the chewing/tapping/pumping tempo.

"Fine," replied The Boss. "Why don't you go first."

"Be glad to," said the Manufacturing Manager, smiling. "Every day people are buying more and more into my message: We simply must improve the Quality of our manufacturing operations."

"If I may play devil's advocate for a moment," said The Boss, "just why is Quality so important to you and your department?"

"Simple: productivity. Productivity's the name of the game in manufacturing—more good stuff out the door, faster. Better Quality means less rework. And less rework means better productivity."

"That's good to hear," said The Boss. "Your objective of increased productivity is certainly of great interest to me. Now, who would like to go next?"

"My answer is really pretty simple," said the Human Resources Manager. "I've gotten everyone to focus their attention on one shared objective: improved morale. It's important that Punctuation Inc. be a sharing, caring place to work, and we can make that happen by improving morale throughout all operations."

"All of that sharing won't slow things down, will it?" asked the Manufacturing Manager.

"Are you insinuating that we all share equally in the costs?" asked the Finance Manager with a shudder.

"You've definitely hit on an important topic with your focus on morale," said The Boss, rescuing the Human Resources Manager. Turning to the Engineering Manager, he said: "And what about your department? Are you making progress with your Quality efforts?"

"Did Maxwell have any equations?" the Engineering Manager responded. "We've made enormous progress toward higher Quality, all driven by one basic realization: All engineers want to work on one and only one project. And of course, you all know which one that is."

"The first one?" said the Manufacturing Manager.

"The lowest-cost one?" said the Finance Manager.

"The leading one?" said the Marketing Manager.

"The same one?" said the Human Resources Manager.

"No," said the Engineering Manager. "You're all wrong. All engineers want to work on the *next* one. We get our kicks by working at the leading edge of technology. By the time we get to working on a project, chances are something newer and more exciting has already begun to come along. So anything that will help us get done with this one and on to the next is most welcome indeed. And by reducing the number of times we have to restudy, rethink, and reengineer problems, better Quality in engineering can help us do that."

"That sounds very good, very exciting," said The Boss. "I can tell you that achieving higher levels of Quality throughout the engineering function in order to keep us at the cutting edge of technology is a matter of the greatest concern to me as well."

"I'm glad to hear that," said the Engineering Manager (not quite hearing exactly what The Boss had said (which is why The Boss had said it exactly the way he had)).

"What about finance? What do you have to tell us about your Quality efforts?" asked The Boss.

"Very simple," replied the Finance Manager. "In the finance department, the bottom line of our Quality efforts is: the bottom line. Quality is flat-out cheaper. Less waste. Less inventory to carry. Smaller buildings to rent. Fewer people to hire. Quality means profit, and profit is why we're in business. That's why Quality is so important to me and my department."

"The last time I looked," said the Engineering Manager, "profit represented the delta between two numbers. And there won't be any numbers to subtract those lower costs from if we aren't getting the technology out the door."

"Ain't *nothing* going out the door—profitably or otherwise—if we can't build it!" said the Manufacturing Manager.

"Studies have shown," said the Marketing Manager, "that there will be nothing to which technology can be applied, nothing to manufacture, and no profits realized if the product has not been effectively targeted to the proper market segment and positioned properly within that segment."

The Human Resources Manager was concerned about the contentiousness in the room. "Before morale begins to suffer," he said, "let's take satisfaction in the fact that this discussion has given us something that we can all share equally: disagreement!"

"I've said it before and I'll say it again," said the Finance Manager. "The bottom line is the bottom line, and Quality can add to it."

"Your point is well taken," said The Boss. Then, turning to the Marketing Manager, he added, "As is yours. Tell me: What do you have to report?"

"Well," she began, "I am pleased to report that of all those reporting to date, I am in the leading position of those naming increased market share as the main objective of their Quality efforts."

"Spoken like a true marketing person," said the Engineering Manager. "It sounded very good, but I'm not quite sure what it meant."

"What it meant is that she went last," said the Manufacturing Manager. "I could sound like I had something different to offer if I knew what everybody else had, too!"

"Differentiation is the essence of marketing," replied the Marketing Manager coolly.

"Please, please, everyone," said The Boss, motioning for silence. "Market share is a critically important issue, and I will be paying great attention to our efforts to gain market share by producing a higher Quality product."

"Thank you," said the Marketing Manager. "You are the only person from that segment of the population that is seated at this table to have understood what I was saying."

The Boss nodded a "you're welcome," all the while thinking to himself that, like the others, she hadn't really understood what *he* was saying.

The Boss continued. "We've heard from all of you as to the focus of your departments' Quality efforts.

"Your main objective," he said to the Manufacturing Manager, "is to improve your department's productivity."

And the Manufacturing Manager nodded (and chewed (and tapped (and pumped))).

"Your main objective," he said to the Human Resources Manager, "is to improve morale."

And the Human Resources Manager nodded.

"Your main objective," he said to the Engineering Manager, "is to work at the cutting edge of technology."

And the Engineering Manager nodded.

"Your main objective," he said to the Finance Manager, "is to increase profits."

And the Finance Manager nodded.

"And your main objective," he said to the Marketing Manager, "is to increase market share."

And the Marketing Manager nodded.

"Well," continued The Boss, "those are certainly important issues. And as I've said all along, I'm extremely interested in the connection between those goals and your Quality efforts. So interested, in fact, that I'd very much like to see those efforts firsthand by paying a visit to each of your departments. And frankly, I can hardly wait. How would tomorrow be for you?"

And the Manufacturing Manager, the Human Resources Manager, the Engineering Manager, the Finance Manager, and the Marketing Manager all nodded.

"Good," said The Boss. "Your enthusiasm is very gratifying. It tells me that we've reached a level of awareness that will enable us to move on to even higher levels of Quality throughout our operations.

"And it's only appropriate that we're talking about these matters in this room. Because it was in this room just a few short months ago that two of the people sitting at this table had the insight that can result in the kind of breakthrough performance we're all after.

"To me, their insight represented the simplest, cleanest statement of the most fundamental Quality problem we face. And I can think of no two better people to express that insight to us than them."

And as he said this, The Boss gestured to the right-hand man and the left-hand man, neither of whom had said a word during the entire meeting and both of whom were flabbergasted that The Boss asked them to speak now.

"You think *we're* best equipped to offer that insight?" asked the right-hand man.

"Absolutely," said The Boss.

"You think *we* understand the fundamental Quality problem we face better than anybody else?" asked the left-hand man.

"Most definitely," said The Boss.

The right-hand man looked at the left-hand man.

The left-hand man looked at the right-hand man.

They turned, in unison, and asked The Boss, "Why???"

To which The Boss replied: *"Exactly!"*

ork lifts whizzed and assembly lines ran and people scurried and machines whirred and whistles blew and people scampered and wheels turned and cranks cranked and people scuttled and it was all a nonstop kaleidoscopic blur of energy and action and noise and controlled frenzy throughout the manufacturing department.

Signs were everywhere, pointing to the Manufacturing Manager's pursuit of higher Quality.

Quality: The Key to Productivity read one.

Higher Quality Means Higher Productivity read another variation on the same theme.

Better Means Faster and Faster Means Better read a third, slightly more oblique exhortation hanging in the assembly area.

Which is where The Boss, the right-hand man, the left-hand man, and the Manufacturing Manager were now in their tour of the manufacturing department.

"We've been making a lot of Quality progress here," said the Manufacturing Manager, gesturing toward a group of workers diligently affixing the little hooks to the bodies of commas.

"Poor Quality here, the hooks fall off. Hooks fall off, commas get rejected. Commas get rejected, one of two things happen: Either they get scrapped, or they get reworked. Either way, productivity goes to pot—and you can't have that in a manufacturing operation!"

"No, no," said the left-hand man.

"Of course you can't," said the right-hand man.

"Well, the problem's gone! We fixed it!" stated the Manufacturing Manager, decisively.

But although his tone was most decisive, the Manufacturing Manager's eyes betrayed just the barest hint of doubt. And although the Manufacturing Manager was oblivious to that slight twinge, The Boss was not.

Just as I thought, thought The Boss.

"That's great news," said The Boss. "Just how did you do it? What are the workers doing now that's caused Quality to go up?"

"Why don't you ask one of them?" said the Manufacturing Manager. "Pick anyone you like. Just don't slow them down."

The Boss approached a worker on the line. "Good morning," he said.

"Morning," answered the assembler, without looking up.

"Tell me," continued The Boss, "just what exactly are you doing?"

"Securing the A-47 precisely 2.35 mm from the C/26-B at an angle of 13 degrees, 7 minutes," he replied mechanically (which also describes the manner in which he was securing the A-47 to the C/26-B).

The Boss chuckled. "You'll have to forgive my ignorance," he said. "But is an A-47 the little hook on the bottom of the comma?"

For the first time, the assembler looked up. "Comma?" he said, quizzically.

The Manufacturing Manager jumped in to clear up the confusion. (There's that twinge again, thought The Boss.) "I decided that the key to Quality was to remove distractions, to get everyone to concentrate completely on the task at hand. We don't waste their time or attention on extraneous stuff like what the final product is, or how it's used. Concentration up, Quality up. Quality up, productivity up!"

"I see," said The Boss.

"Shall we move on to the last area in the department?" asked the Manufacturing Manager. And without waiting for an answer, he led the tour group (at civil defense alert pace) over to the painting area.

"Good morning," said The Boss, approaching a worker directly.

"Morning," said the painter, not looking up.

"So this is the painting area, right?" continued The Boss.

"Right," said the painter, concentrating fully on the task at hand.

"If this is the last area in the department," asked The Boss, "where do the pieces go from here when you're done painting them?"

"Don't know," replied the painter, at last looking up. "All I know is that it's my job to do a Quality job of painting. That's what's important to me. Leastwise, that's what's important to him." And as she said this, she pointed her paintbrush toward the Manufacturing Manager.

"We spare them those distractions," explained the Manufacturing Manager proudly (but not without yet another twinge—another twinge noticed by The Boss). "That way they're more likely to get it right the first time. 'Get it right the first time, get more done all the time!' I always say."

"Indeed," said The Boss, noncommittally. Then he glanced at his watch. "We have to be moving along. But before we go, I want to thank you very much for the tour of your department. It's very clear to me that some of the key Quality messages haven't been lost on you."

"Yes, thank you," said the right-hand man.

"Thank you, yes," said the left-hand man.

"You're very welcome," said the Manufacturing Manager, as he ushered them through the doors leading out of the manufacturing department.

"I have to admit," he added, "that when you began a lot of this Quality stuff, I was a skeptic. I thought it would just get in the way of the real business of running a business. But now I'm a believer: Quality has gone up and productivity has gone up. And that's the name of the game back in there," he said, with a quick jerk of his thumb back toward the manufacturing area. (The right-hand man and left-hand man followed his pointing thumb to a sign on the wall over the doors they had just passed through, which read: *Productivity's the name of the game back in there!*)

"That message," said The Boss, taking note of the sign, "is pretty hard to miss. In fact, it's also pretty clear the workers in your department haven't missed it."

"Thanks," said the Manufacturing Manager, oblivious to the purposeful ambiguity in The Boss's tone.

"I'll let you get back to your work," said The Boss, nodding toward the doorway. "After all," he added, good-naturedly, "I don't want to hold up productivity!"

The Manufacturing Manager fairly exploded back through the door, shouting an additional "Thanks!" back over his shoulder.

"Well," said The Boss to the left-hand man and the right-hand man, "they're doing a lot of the correct things in there."

"Yes, they are," agreed the right-hand man.

"Indeed they are," added the left-hand man.

Having let out enough rope, The Boss calmly continued: "It's just too bad that it isn't going to work."

There followed a two-beat pause.

"It *isn't?*" asked the right-hand man and the left-hand man.

"No, it isn't," said The Boss.

"Why?" asked the right-hand man and the left-hand man.

"Exactly!" said The Boss. "I never cease to be impressed at your insightfulness!"

The right-hand man and the left-hand man beamed. They were pleased that The Boss was so impressed. They would have been more pleased if they understood why.

Come to think of it, so would The Boss.

’m just thrilled to have you here visiting our department!” said the Human Resources Manager to The Boss as he met him at the entrance to the human resources department. Then, turning quickly to the right-hand man and the left-hand man, he added, “Of course, no more thrilled than I am about the fact that the two of you were able to join us. Nor less so, either. I am, as it happens, precisely equally thrilled that *all three* of you are here!”

“Thank you,” said The Boss, speaking for all three of them. “What do you have to show us? Just what is the focus of your Quality program?”

“Well,” said the Human Resources Manager, leading them down a hallway, “it’s our job to deal with Quality as it pertains to the people who work here. And isn’t it axiomatic that it’s more economical to build the Quality in than to find defects after the fact and repair them?”

“Yes,” said The Boss, obviously

pleased that the Human Resources Manager had so well "internalized" (The Boss always thought thoughts like that while in the human resources department) his Quality message, "it is."

"So," said the Human Resources Manager, "we decided that to "design" Quality into our employees, we should focus our attention on the earliest possible point in the process: new employee orientation."

"Just what did the new employee orientation process look like before your Quality program?" asked the right-hand man.

"It wasn't much," said the Human Resources Manager. "We had them sign a couple of insurance forms, gave them a copy of the week's cafeteria menu, and sent them off to their desks."

"Doesn't sound like a Quality orientation program to me," agreed the left-hand man.

"I'll say," said the Human Resources Manager. "It got most people started off with a bad taste in their mouths. That was un-Quality in the extreme. And that led to serious morale problems, which, when you get right down to it, is what really matters."

The foursome turned a corner and found themselves facing a door over which had been mounted a sign reading: *Orientation.*

"Aha!" exulted the Human Resources Manager. "Here we are!"

He opened the door, extending his left arm, palm up, in a shall-we-go-in gesture.

And so they did.

Inside, the new, high-Quality orientation treatment of which the Human Resources Manager was so proud was just beginning for twelve new Punctuation Inc. employees.

"Welcome," began the facilitator to the new-hires, "to Punctuation Inc. I, personally, am very glad that you will be working here." Spotting the four visitors who had just entered at the back of the room, she added, "But I am no more glad than are any of Punctuation Inc.'s employees. Am I right?"

"Absolutely," said The Boss, in total sincerity. "We're all equally glad to have you all as part of the Punctuation Inc. family."

"Yes, that's right," continued the facilitator. "We want this to be a nice place for you to work because . . . well, what more is needed than that—because we want this to be a nice place to work!"

The new employees smiled.

So did The Boss (albeit a tad anxiously).

The orientation program went on in this same warm, comfortable, indefatigably *nice* vein for the next 45 minutes.

First a slide show was shown showing slides of happy Punctuation Inc. employees.

Then scores of happy Punctuation Inc.

employees were marched past the front of the room: a beaming parade of unremitting job satisfaction.

Poems written by employees, describing their level of contentment (very high) with their jobs, were read aloud.

The brand-new (as part of the new orientation package) company song ("It's So Nice to Have a Nice Place to Work!") was sung:

> It's so nice to have a nice place to
>   work!
> 'Cause there's no point then to malin-
>   ger or to shirk!
> There's a niceness, oh, so rare,
> That fills up each breath of air,
> Oh, it's so nice to have a nice place to
>   work!

Clearly, it seemed that the new Punctuation Inc. high-Quality orientation session was going according to the Human Resources Manager's plan.

He leaned over and whispered to The Boss: "I must admit that I was a bit of a skeptic about a lot of the Quality stuff that you've been preaching. But I look at this room, and now I'm convinced. 'You've got to design the Quality in,' you've been saying. And you're right. By designing the Quality into our orientation package, we'll get the kind of morale we're after right from the beginning."

The last strains of the company song filled the air: "Oh, it's so nice to have a nice place to work!"

"Excellent job!" crowed the facilitator. "You all did a wonderful job of singing! Now, as a last order of business, I'd be happy to answer any questions that any of you might have. Yes?"

A small man in the front row stood. "What do we make here?"

"Why," replied the facilitator, "we make friends!"

"No," said the small man, with a smile, "I mean what does the company make?"

"Oh, the *company!*" said the facilitator, beaming her new understanding of the small man's question. "Why, we make people happy!"

"No, no," said the small man. "What do the people who work here do while they're on the job?"

"Why," replied the facilitator, gamely, "we fulfill our potentials by sharing in meaningful workplace experiences."

"What," persevered the small man, his smile now fully gone, "is the product which Punctuation Inc. produces and then offers for sale in the open market?!?"

"Oh, so *that's* what you wanted to know?" said the facilitator, with a hollow chuckle. "I'm sorry. I'm not a technical type. You'll have to ask your supervisor to answer that question for you, okay?"

When The Boss heard this, his eyes

shifted quickly to the Human Resources Manager's eyes. They saw what The Boss expected to see: that same, slight, imperceptible-to-anyone-who-isn't-The-Boss twinge.

Ever more certain that his conclusions about Punctuation Inc.'s Quality problems were correct, The Boss quietly scribbled a brief note and just as quietly passed it to the right-hand man and the left-hand man.

The note read:

Questions like the one the small man just asked can be very key to our quality efforts.

Having read the note, the left-hand man and the right-hand man looked at each other in silence.

Then, looking back to The Boss, they both mouthed the same question, also in silence: "Why?"

"Exactly!" mouthed The Boss in response. "Exactly!"

he first thing the Finance Manager did after greeting The Boss, the right-hand man, and the left-hand man was to insert a card into a gray metal box mounted on the wall just inside the door to the finance department.

Ka-*chunkkkk!*

"Is that a time clock?" asked the right-hand man, uncertainly.

"Yes."

"You mean *you* have to punch a time clock every day?" asked the left-hand man, incredulously.

"Oh, no, no, no!" said the Finance Manager, laughing.

The left-hand and right-hand men seemed relieved, but still confused.

"Well, then, what's it for?"

"I use it to make sure that the amount I charge back to you for the time I spend with you is accurate," said the Finance Manager, adding, without the slightest hint of irony, "I think it would be unreasonable to do otherwise."

The Boss's attention had been captured by a worker who was sawing off a section of a long, skinny, yellow extrusion: it looked for all the world like an incredibly long pencil.

"What," asked The Boss, pointing, "is that person doing?"

"She's sawing a section off of an incredibly long pencil," answered the Finance Manager matter-of-factly. "You can buy them in bulk, you know. It's silly to have to pay someone else to cut them into little eight-inch lengths for you. I mean, who decided that eight inches was the perfect length for a pencil, anyway?"

"What about the little erasers that come on the end of precut pencils?" asked the left-hand man.

"What do people do when they make mistakes?" asked the right-hand man.

The Finance Manager had a ready answer. "If I've learned one thing from The Boss's preaching about Quality, it's that mistakes cost money. It's cheaper to do things right. Better Quality means better profitability, and, well, what could be better than that?"

"But," pressed The Boss, "mistakes *do* happen! What do people do then?"

"They go and see Junior."

"Who's Junior?" asked the right-hand man and the left-hand man in unison.

"Junior is the person who will rent them

an eraser to fix their mistakes," replied the Finance Manager.

"*Rent* them an eraser?" asked the left-hand man and the right-hand man in unison.

"Yes, rent them an eraser."

"Don't people feel just a little bit foolish when they have to do that?" asked The Boss.

"Of course!" said the Finance Manager. "You told us that most Quality problems are built into the system. So I decided that the lowest-cost way to run the department would be to improve Quality by designing a system whereby defects will be prevented from occurring in the first place."

"So," said The Boss, seeing the light, "since people feel foolish at having to rent an eraser, they will be more careful about making mistakes in the first place."

"Precisely!" said the Finance Manager.

"But what about Junior's salary?" asked the left-hand man.

"Doesn't that offset the cost savings?" asked the right-hand man.

The Finance Manager smiled: "The reason we call him Junior is that he's a high school junior working here as an intern. His 'salary' is the invaluable experience he's gaining by seeing firsthand the inner workings of a modern, sophisticated finance department. Finance is Junior's life; at least that's what he told me when I interviewed him."

"I'd like to meet Junior," said The Boss.

"Of course," said the Finance Manager, leading the group over to Junior's desk.

"Junior," said the Finance Manager, "I'd like you to meet The Boss."

Junior stood and extended his right hand to The Boss. But before he did, he slipped a card into the time clock affixed to the side of his desk: ka-*chunkkk!*

"Don't worry," said Junior, seeing The Boss's surprise. "You'll get a chargeback statement, but it will be at my salary rate of $0.00 per hour. I'm a reasonable man."

The Finance Manager looked as though he were about to burst with pride. "Come with me this way," he said, leading The Boss by the arm. "I'd like to show you another Quality project we've got going."

"This way" turned out to be the invoicing area, where row upon row of people were stuffing itemized bills into envelopes and sending them out through the mail.

"My goodness!" gasped the left-hand man. "You certainly have a lot of people sending out invoices!"

"Is business really that good?" gasped the right-hand man.

"I can't say as I know," said the Finance Manager. "But what I *do* know is that it's, net, cheaper for us to do it this way."

"What do you mean when you say 'this way'?" asked The Boss.

"Well," began the Finance Manager, "as you know, Punctuation Inc. has several different product lines." Picking up an order form out of a pile on one of the workers' desks, he continued, "For example, here's an order for 5,000 exclamation points from our Strident line; 10,000 periods from our Decisive line; 3,000 asterisks from our Footnote line; and 3,500 commas from our Filigree line. We used to send out just one invoice for an order like this."

"So what?" asked the right-hand man and the left-hand man.

"So it cost us a lot of money, that's so what!" replied the Finance Manager, a tad sharply. "Do you realize what that did to us when the payment arrived? A single payment for all four product lines? It wreaked havoc on our accounting systems, that's what happened!

"Mistakes got made! Revenues got posted to the wrong product lines! That cost the company money! That cost my people money! But I'm a reasonable man: If someone showed me that the problem came from our old invoicing system, Junior gave them a cut rate on the eraser rental."

"You said 'the old system,'" said The Boss. "I take that to mean you now have a new system?"

"Yes, we do," said the Finance Manager. "That's why we've got so many people here in invoicing. Now, instead of sending out just one bill for all four products on the order, we send out four separate bills. That way, when the payments come in, they've already been sorted out by product line. Fewer mistakes, higher Quality, lower costs: just like The Boss said."

"How long have you been using the new system?" asked The Boss.

"About a month."

"And has it been working as you anticipated?" asked The Boss.

"Let's ask Junior," replied the Finance Manager, confidently leading them back to Junior's desk. "After all, improved Quality would show up in the eraser rental figures."

Upon arriving, the Finance Manager said, "Junior, The Boss has a question for you."

"Yes, Junior, I was wondering—"
Ka-*chunkkkk!*

"—whether you had seen any improvement in Quality as a result of the new invoicing system."

"Oh, yes, yes," said Junior. "Eraser rental fees are off by almost 50 percent. Quality has definitely improved."

"There's the proof!" exulted the Finance Manager. "Hard, quantifiable proof!"

But the Finance Manager's exultation was surprisingly short-lived.

"Is something the matter?" asked The Boss (who suspected that he knew exactly what the matter was).

"No, not really," replied the Finance Manager. "It's just that . . . well, with the new system, there's a lot more paperwork per order. So I kind of expected that we'd make up for the dropoff in eraser rentals by an increase in paper clip sales."

"Yes," said The Boss. "I suppose that makes sense."

"But it just hasn't happened," came the Finance Manager's twinge-tinged comment, "and I don't understand why."

"Exactly," muttered The Boss, under his breath. "Exactly."

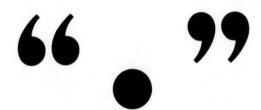

he Boss stuck his head into the office of the Engineering Manager, with the right-hand man and left-hand man close behind him.

"Is this," asked The Boss, "a good time for our Quality tour?"

Looking up from her desk, the Engineering Manager replied, "Does f equal ma?"

She came around to the front of her desk and greeted her guests effusively. "If I were given to imprecision," she began, "I would say that I can't begin to tell you how excited I am about the progress we've made on Quality here in the engineering department. But I'm not, and I can, so I can't."

And difficult though it may be to believe, The Boss, the right-hand man, and the left-hand man understood her *perfectly*!

The Boss said as much. "I'm just amazed that I understood exactly what you told us!"

"So am I!" said the left-hand man.

"So am I!" said the right-hand man.

Her point made, the Engineering Manager smiled. "That's because the Quality of the Punctuation Marks that I was using was so good. You see, we recently had an engineering breakthrough which enabled us to increase the information density per piece of punctuation *without* causing any overheating problems! A technological breakthrough resulting from improved Quality of the engineering process. Without it, we'd still be building prototypes."

"That would have been bad," said the right-hand man.

"No," replied the Engineering Manager. "That would have been good. When you're prototyping, you're not quite there yet. And that's where the fun is in engineering. But because of the improved Quality, we were able to move beyond prototyping that much more quickly."

"Well, that's good," said the left-hand man.

"No," replied the Engineering Manager. "That's bad. Once you get beyond prototyping, you move into routine production. And no engineer wants to get stuck doing that kind of work. Everybody wants to get on to the next one."

"That's bad," said the right-hand man, taking a wild stab.

"No it's not," countered the left-hand man, also taking a shot at it, "it's good."

The Engineering Manager let them both down: "Personally, I don't know whether it's good or bad. All I know is that it's the way it is in engineering. And that's why Quality is so important to us. By improving the Quality of the work we do, we reduce the amount of rework. And with less rework, everyone can get done with this one and on to the next one that much quicker."

"And that's what most people are really interested in?" asked The Boss.

"Was Newton interested in apples?" replied the Engineering Manager. "Here, let me show you. Let's go take a look at what my top engineer is up to."

The Boss, the left-hand man, the right-hand man, and the Engineering Manager moved toward an industrious-looking fellow working at a bench at the back of the room. On top of the bench was a fish tank full of water. And in the water floated a broad and apparently random selection of punctuation marks.

"This," began the Engineering Manager, not wanting to disturb her ace engineer, "is some work he had been doing in underwater punctuation marks. It was based on the principle that sound travels better under water than it does through the air. So that, for example, the incremental energy added to a sentence by an exclamation point would have a compounding effect under water." (The right-hand man and left-hand man nodded sagely. Neither had the faintest idea what the Engineering Manager was talking about.)

"With proper work, a single noise, made once, could be made to replenish itself. Once that's been done, all you have to do is convert that noise into a standing wave, focus it, and bingo! The second law of thermodynamics is repealed: The energy crisis is over!"

"That's great!" said the left-hand man.

"No, I'm afraid not," said the Engineering Manager. "Technology waits for no one. While we were in the development stages, somebody else leapfrogged us . . . came out with a more advanced version."

"That's too bad," said the right-hand man.

"No, that's good," said the Engineering Manager. "The only thing that moves faster than technology is the regulatory industry. No sooner had the advanced version come out than it had been legislated out of practicality."

"That's a fascinating story," said The Boss. "Just how long ago did all of this happen?"

The Engineering Manager interrupted the engineer to relay The Boss's question: "Just how long ago did all of that happen?"

"That's a tough one to answer. It seems so long ago," said the engineer.

"Approximately?" asked the Engineering Manager.

"Oh, I don't know. Around ten-twenty-nine, I suppose."

"You mean all of this happened since last October 29?" asked The Boss, surprised at how truly fast things moved.

"No," replied the engineer. "Since ten-twenty-nine *this morning*. Last October 29 was the Stone Age when it comes to punctuation technology."

The Boss was amazed. Turning to the Engineering Manager, he asked, "Do things really move *that* fast?"

"Does entropy always go up?" replied the Engineering Manager. "That's why Quality is so important to us, why we've focused our Quality efforts on the process of developing new products—so we'll stay out of situations like that on the next one."

"Speaking of which," said The Boss, directing his attention to the hard-at-work engineer, "what are you working on?"

"Digital question marks."

"Hmmm," replied The Boss, "that's interesting. But why digital question marks?"

"?" said the engineer's look, putting an experimental digital question mark to use.

"What about nuance . . . shadings of meaning . . . subtlety?" asked The Boss.

With digital punctuation technology, there is no such thing as a question lingering in the air and fading gradually away: It's either being asked or not asked. So the engineer had to put a second digital question mark to use.

"?" said his expression.

"Let me explain," offered the Engineering Manager. "It's a matter of focus. Our focus is technology. We need to spend our time answering questions like *what* (What should we build? What can we make the technology do?) and *how* (How can we make it? How big? How fast?), not *why*.

"That kind of focus will give us higher Quality in the process of developing new products. And higher Quality in that process means we can get on to the next one sooner. That's always the objective for the people around here . . . the *next* one."

"But isn't that a recipe for frustration?" asked the right-hand man.

"How do you mean?"

"Well, once they get on to the next one," asked the left-hand man, "don't all of their instincts make them want to go on to the *next* next one, and then the next, and then the next?"

"I suppose so," said the Engineering Manager, with an ever-so-slight twinge.

"And you say your people thrive under such conditions?" asked the right-hand man and the left-hand man. "Why?"

"Because that's what it means to be an engineer," replied the Engineering Manager with a shrug. "And besides, like I said, we don't ask why."

Exactly, thought The Boss. Exactly.

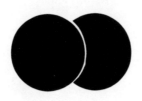

think it's safe to say," said the Marketing Manager to The Boss, the left-hand man, and the right-hand man, who were making their fifth (and final) department visit of the day, "that we in the marketing department are strategically positioned to provide a perspective on Quality that is unsurpassed in the company.

"Why do you say that?" tested The Boss (although he was pretty sure he knew what her answer would be).

"Because it's our job to promote, sell, and distribute our products. If Quality is good, then that job is a lot easier and market share goes up. If Quality is bad, forget it. Hardly seems fair, does it? I mean, being so affected by something over which you have no control?"

The right-hand man and the left-hand man nodded at the apparent good sense of what the Marketing Manager had said.

The Boss nodded, too, but for a different reason. His suspicion had been correct.

"But that hasn't stopped us from taking

The Boss's Quality message to heart!" said the Marketing Manager. "In fact, a recent study shows that we were the first department to formally undertake a Quality program, plus or minus two departments."

"My, how . . . interesting," equivocated The Boss. "Why don't you show us the way to the Quality project you have in the works?"

"I'll be glad to," said the Marketing Manager. "It has to do with our new, ultra-high-Quality semicolon. Come with me."

And with that she led them to the office of her lead marketing specialist. "Our lead marketing specialist," said the Marketing Manager, "will now give us a dog-and-pony show."

"A what?" asked the right-hand man.

"You know," explained the Marketing Manager. "An overview of the mind share that we're trying to occupy."

"Pardon me?" asked the left-hand man.

"He's going to review the marketing plans for the new semicolon," translated The Boss. Then, turning to the marketing specialist, he said, "Proceed."

"We've decided to build a key piece of the introduction of the product around a new pricing strategy," began the marketing specialist. "It just seems to make logical sense that the price of a semicolon ought to be half the price of a colon—of comparable Quality, of course. Quality is always an issue to be dealt with here in marketing. But pricing is not all there is to our introduction plan. This is a serious, complex business. Packaging is important, too—which is what *this* is for."

And with that, the marketing specialist withdrew a small, brushed-leather carrying case, featuring an excruciatingly tasteful debossing of the Punctuation Inc. logo.

"A recent study shows that a 58 percent share of the marketplace would prefer carrying their semicolons in a brushed-leather carrying case rather than stuffing them into the slots of their penny loafers," said the marketing specialist. "And if this baby could talk," he continued, gazing admiringly at the carrying case, "she'd say one word: Quality!"

"Talk is cheap," muttered The Boss, disapprovingly.

"What?" asked the Marketing Manager, anxiously.

"Oh," recovered The Boss, slightly flustered that his disapproval had slipped out, "I said, 'Chalk the Jeep!' 'It's an old Army expression . . . motor pool, you know. It means 'That one's the winner!' "

"Oh!" beamed the Marketing Manager, relieved. Turning to the marketing specialist, she said, "Carry on!"

"I've saved the best for last," he said, warming to the occasion. "Whoever said 'Build a better mousetrap and the world will beat a path to your door' didn't know anything about marketing. You've got to *tell* them you've got a better mousetrap before you can gain mousetrap market share. And that means advertising!"

The marketing specialist removed a large piece of pasteboard from behind his desk. Pausing dramatically for effect, he proclaimed, "Behold! The new ad campaign!"

Mounted on the pasteboard were three artist's sketches of advertisements.

The first one showed a picture of a very large truck—a semi—under the headline:

> *There's Nothing "Semi"*
> *About Our Quality:*
> *Buy Punctuation Inc. Semicolons!*

The second one showed a loaf of bread, one side of which was thoroughly cooked and one side of which was still doughy, under the headline:

> *There's Nothing Half-Baked*
> *About Our Quality:*
> *Buy Punctuation Inc. Semicolons!*

The third one showed a sketch of the 50-yard line on a football field, under the headline:

> *There's Nothing Halfway*
> *About Our Quality:*
> *Buy Punctuation Inc. Semicolons!*

The marketing specialist eagerly awaited his audience's reaction.

The right-hand man and the left-hand man could not contain their excitement. "Chalk the Jeep!" they shouted.

"Yes," said The Boss, grateful for the cue (although he had grave reservations about the ad campaign, he knew he had to let things proceed at their own pace), "Chalk the Jeep!"

The marketing specialist fairly glowed with pleasure. "Do you really mean it?" he asked, somewhat self-consciously fishing for further assurance.

"Oh, yes!" said The Boss, disingenuously. "I can honestly say that never have I more appropriately uttered those words. Congratulations!"

At that final, gleeful note, there were handshakes all around as The Boss, the right-hand man, and the left-hand man said their good-byes and thanked their hosts for the presentation.

"Come back again," said the Marketing Manager. "We'd be glad to show you how big a part Quality has to play here in helping the marketing department stake out higher market share any time. I only wish it were something over which we had some control."

As the Marketing Manager said this, The Boss noticed that by-now-familiar twinge. But he said nothing about it as he completed the farewell ritual.

Once out of the marketing department, the left-hand man whispered something to the right-hand man, who nodded.

Then the right-hand man whispered something to the left-hand man, who nodded.

"Are you going to share your little secret with me," asked The Boss, "or do I have to guess?"

"It's not a secret," said the right-hand man.

"It's just that we've just surveyed each other," said the left-hand man, "and discovered that 100 percent of those questioned are puzzled about the same thing."

"And what might that be?" asked The Boss.

"Well, there was one thing you'd expect to hear a lot about in a marketing department, but it never came up," said the right-hand man.

"And what is that?" asked The Boss (who knew exactly what "it" was).

"Not one word was said about customers," said the left-hand man.

"Hmmm," said The Boss, contemplatively. "Interesting notion. And you were wondering, perhaps, why?"

"Exactly!" said the right-hand man and the left-hand man.

And with that, The Boss allowed himself a small amount of satisfaction at the skill with which he had led them to their insight.

Chalk the Jeep, he thought to himself, a little smile barely visible. Chalk the Jeep.

want to begin," The Boss announced, beginning his weekly staff meeting, "by giving you all my special thanks for your hospitality last week in showing me and my right-hand and left-hand men around the various Quality projects you have going."

"Yes," added the right-hand man and the left-hand man. "Thank you."

The Manufacturing Manager, the Human Resources Manager, the Finance Manager, the Engineering Manager, and the Marketing Manager all smiled their you're welcomes.

The Boss continued: "I really appreciate all of the hard work and energy you've been putting into those Quality efforts. It's been very gratifying to see all of you embracing the fundamental importance of Quality and focusing your efforts in such different and creative ways.

"To see you," he said to the Manufacturing Manager, "dealing with our fundamental Quality problem by focusing on productivity."

And the Manufacturing Manager nodded (and chewed (and tapped (and pumped))) his thanks.

"To see you," said The Boss to the Human Resources Manager, "deal with our fundamental Quality problem by focusing on morale."

"I am as gratified by your thanks as you are by my efforts," responded the Human Resources Manager, warmly.

"To see you," said The Boss to the Finance Manager, "dealing with our fundamental Quality problem by focusing on profitability."

"I'm the richer for it," responded the Finance Manager, economically.

"To see you," said The Boss to the Engineering Manager, "dealing with our fundamental Quality problem by focusing on technology."

"Your leadership has not been without its breakthrough elements for us," responded the Engineering Manager, precisely.

"And finally," said The Boss, turning to the Marketing Manager, "to see you dealing with our fundamental Quality problem by focusing on market share."

"I'm pleased to announce the results of a sampling of opinions I've just taken which shows that five out of five people surveyed are happy to have been at your service," responded the Marketing Manager, flashing a winning smile.

"Well, I thank you all again," said The Boss, "and I'm sure my right-hand man and left-hand man will agree that our Quality problems are all but solved, won't you?"

"Oh, yes," said the left-hand man, with a slight twinge.

"Oh, absolutely," said the right-hand man, similarly twinged.

The Boss couldn't have been more pleased. He sensed that a seminal moment in the history of Punctuation Inc. was upon him. After all the problems, and all the hard work, and all the disappointments, and all the worries and frustration and anguish, he was about to get at what he was now utterly convinced was at the very innermost heart of the matter.

"Your words say 'yes' but your eyes don't seem so sure," said The Boss to the right-hand man and the left-hand man. "Is something troubling you?"

The left-hand man spoke first.

"It's just that . . . well . . ."

"Yes, go ahead. Say what's on your mind," The Boss said kindly. (Don't let me down now, he thought. Three months ago I said that you had a key role to play in this little drama, and you're on *now*!)

The left-hand man seemed to sense The Boss's support. "You all talk about your different approaches to our 'fundamental' Quality problem," he said to the five operations managers. "But if those approaches are all so different, then maybe the problem you're solving isn't so fundamental—at least not from Punctuation Inc.'s perspective, anyway."

Then the right-hand man spoke. "Yes . . . and . . . well . . ."

"Go ahead," said The Boss, soothingly. "Say it." (The next line is yours, he thought.)

The right-hand man's resolve steadied. "You all talk about focusing on Quality in five different ways," he said to the five operating managers, "but it seems to me that five different focuses add up to no focus at all."

,,, ... ??? !!!
,,, ... ??? !!!

,,, ... ??? !!!
,,, ... ??? !!!

,,, ... ??? !!!
,,, ... ??? !!!

,,, ... ??? !!!
,,, ... ??? !!!

The room fell very silent.

(Bravo! thought The Boss. You've played your roles magnificently!)

"Interesting observations," mused The Boss out loud. "Interesting." Then, turning to his operating managers, he asked, "What do you all think of their observations?"

"I think their observations are unproductive," said the Manufacturing Manager. "But then, a little time spent working closer to the assembly line would clear up their thinking."

"I think their observations are most disturbing," said the Human Resources Manager. "But then, a little time spent working closer to people would show them the light."

"I think their observations are unprofitable," said the Finance Manager. "But then, it's nothing that a little more exposure to the bottom line wouldn't clear up."

"I think their observations are illogical," said the Engineering Manager. "But then, freshmen can't solve differential equations on the first day of class."

"I think their observations are losers," said the Marketing Manager. "And a recent study," she added, looking around the table to see the Finance Manager, the Human Resources Manager, the Manufacturing Manager, and the Engineering Manager all nodding as if on cue, "shows that a 100 percent share of those surveyed would agree."

The right-hand man and left-hand man receded back into their seats like little right-hand and left-hand boys.

Dejected.

Depressed.

Defeated.

And when The Boss cleared his throat to speak, they braced themselves for even worse.

"I think . . ." said The Boss, in tantalizingly slow, measured tones, "that their observations . . ."

The Boss metronomically turned his gaze from manager—

"represent . . ."

—to manager—

"the most insightful . . ."

—to manager—

"the most enlightened . . ."

—to manager—

"the most important observations made at Punctuation Inc. since our Quality problem began."

The right-hand man's and left-hand man's emotions shifted from despair to elation.

The room fell very, very silent.

The Boss (being The Boss) seized the moment.

Turning abruptly to the Manufacturing Manager he said, "Beyond productivity, *why* do you suppose Quality is so important?"

Without waiting for an answer, he turned to the Human Resources Manager, and asked, "Beyond morale, *why* do you suppose Quality is so important?"

And to the Finance Manager: "Beyond profitability, *why* do you suppose Quality is so important?"

And to the Engineering Manager: "Beyond technology, *why?*"

And to the Marketing Manager: "Beyond market share, *why?*"

Then, to all of them: "Why? *Fundamentally—WHY?*"

The Boss let the question hover like a cloud (a phenomenon made possible by his use of a standard analog question mark).

Then he spoke in a very firm, very direct tone.

"I'm concerned that we still haven't got it, still haven't grasped the essence of our problem. So I'm going to ask you all to go back and give some thought to that question, give some thought to Why."

Not only was The Boss's tone very firm and very direct; it was also very unusual for The Boss. So unusual, in fact, that the others were taken aback by it.

Just as The Boss had intended.

The Manufacturing Manager spoke first. "You want us," he said, "to spend time figuring out *why* in addition to all of the other work we're doing? Over and above the Quality projects you've asked for from us?"

"Yes," said The Boss, very firmly and directly, "I do."

"If my analysis is correct," said the Engineering Manager, "surely you must know the answer to Why. Is that not so?"

"Yes," said The Boss, very firmly, very directly, "I do know the answer."

"Well, then," said the Human Resources Manager, "why don't you simply share it with the rest of us?"

"I could do that," said The Boss, very firmly, very directly, "but I'm afraid you wouldn't understand."

"What I do understand," said the Finance Manager, "is that the time spent solving your riddle will cost us—will cost *you*—a bundle in chargebacks."

"It's a price I'm most willing to pay," said The Boss, very firmly, very directly.

It pained The Boss to behave in such an arbitrary, condescending way. But he was, after all, The Boss, and it was something he knew he *had* to do.

"I'm sorry to have to report," said the Marketing Manager, glumly, "that in the last five minutes you have dramatically lost share in the marketplace of ideas."

The silence in the room approached ear-splitting levels.

Then a very angry Manufacturing Manager began to speak. "I have to say that I resent this," he said, resentfully. "You're asking us to take on extra work . . . work that you *say* is so important . . . and you can't—you *won't!*—tell us why. And that forces me to ask that same question of you: Why? Why is Why so important?"

"Why?" asked the Human Resources Manager.

"Why?" asked the Finance Manager.

"Why?" asked the Engineering Manager.

"Why?" asked the Marketing Manager.

The Boss let out a long, slow breath (the better to let them all consider the question they had just asked).

"Thank you," he said, "for your passion and your openness." He paused again, then said, "Maybe you're right. Maybe I ought to just tell you why."

And with that, The Boss got up from the conference table and walked over to the file cabinet next to his desk. Reaching inside, he pulled out a large brown sack.

"A little more than three months ago," he said as he walked back over to the conference table, "we thought we had our Quality problems solved. We were happy, exuberant, proud of ourselves. So proud, in fact, that one day, when a customer came in to see me, I assumed that he had come to give me his thanks for providing him with such high-Quality products.

"Well, he gave me something, all right. He gave me this."

And then The Boss tipped the large brown sack and poured a pile of punctuation marks—Punctuation Inc.'s punctuation marks—onto the conference table, just as the disgruntled customer had done so many weeks before.

Periods.
Semicolons.
Question marks.
Ellipses.
Dashes.
Parentheses.
Brackets.
Apostrophes.
Asterisks.

You name it, they all poured out of the sack into a dusty black heap.

Finally, one last question mark fell out of the sack . . .

rolled down the side of the dusty black heap . . .

skipped across the width of the conference table . . .

and came to rest at the edge of the table, right next to where The Boss was standing.

"This," said The Boss, pointing to the dusty black heap, "is Why.

"Why? Because we apparently hadn't solved our Quality problem. Because we hadn't delivered the value for which a customer had paid us. Because we had let a customer down.

"It's just that simple. It's just that complicated."

, , ,　· · ·　? ? ?　! ! !
, , ,　· · ·　? ? ?　! ! !
, , ,　· · ·　? ? ?　! ! !
, , ,　· · ·　? ? ?　! ! !

, , ,　· · ·　? ? ?　! ! !
, , ,　· · ·　? ? ?　! ! !
, , ,　· · ·　? ? ?　! ! !
, , ,　· · ·　? ? ?　! ! !

, , ,　· · ·　? ? ?　! ! !
, , ,　· · ·　? ? ?　! ! !
, , ,　· · ·　? ? ?　! ! !
, , ,　· · ·　? ? ?　! ! !

The Boss paused, looking from face to face at the conference table.

"I have a suggestion for all of you . . . that you spend a little less time focusing inward on our own, internal concerns, and a little more time focusing outward, thinking about our customers' concerns."

"You mean," said the Manufacturing Manager, "that you want us to reconstruct our Quality programs?"

"To reorient our thinking?" said the Human Resources Manager.

"To write off our efforts to date?" said the Finance Manager.

"To get back to the basic laws of the business universe?" said the Engineering Manager.

"To think in terms of the individuals that make up the marketplace rather than the marketplace as a whole?" said the Marketing Manager.

"All in order to focus on the *customer?*" said all five.

"Yes," said The Boss. Very firmly, very directly.

"*Why?*" said all five.

"Exactly!" shouted The Boss with delight.

And as he shouted his delighted shout, he brought his palm—*whappp!!*—crashing onto the conference table.

And the dusty black heap was catapulted into a smoky gray cloud, levitating over the table.

And when the cloud had settled back down, something very, very interesting had happened.

Directly in front of each of the operating managers, a single exclamation point had fallen.

And when they saw the exclamation point—with the question Why still hovering in the air—they all put their exclamation points to use . . .

And, at the same instant, all five of them understood what The Boss had been up to for the past three months.

And they all smiled.

Exactly, thought The Boss. Exactly.

aving said his good-byes in his outer office to his operating managers, The Boss reentered his office, closing the door behind him.

"Well!" he began, turning his attention to his right-hand man and left-hand man, who were still seated at the conference table. "That couldn't have gone much better, don't you think?"

After a slight (but noticeable-to-The-Boss) pause, they answered.

"Oh, no . . . my, no," said the right-hand man.

"Couldn't have been any better," said the left-hand man.

The Boss decided on the direct approach.

"You still haven't *quite* got it, have you?" he asked. But because his tone was solicitous, not challenging, they were more than ready to answer.

"It seems that we *should* have gotten it," said the left-hand man.

"I mean, after all, you told them that we were right," said the right-hand man.

"But everybody understands—" said the left-hand man.

"Except us!" said the right-hand man.

The Boss had known all along that he would have to have this conversation with them, so he was ready.

"First of all," he began, kindly, "there is no reason for you to be embarrassed about not seeing things quite as clearly as the others. There's no way you could have, operating from a staff position. That's perfectly consistent with my theory."

"Theory?" asked the right-hand man.

"What theory?" asked the left-hand man.

"The theory that I've been operating under ever since the night that that customer dumped out his large brown sack of punctuation marks onto my desk: Theory Why."

The right-hand man and left-hand man were more confused than ever.

"Let me explain," continued The Boss. "Way back at the beginning, when Process Inc. first began to show up in our monthly reports, we spent all of our time and energy trying to figure out What our problem was. We had many meetings, many discussions. I conducted extensive market research. And finally we had an answer to What: We had a Quality problem."

The right-hand man and left-hand man nodded.

"That was very good, very important. It

represented very real progress," said The Boss. "So, having answered What, we then took what seemed to be the next logical step: We know What our problem is, so How do we fix it?

"Our first response to How was simple exhortation. But that didn't work because people thought that we were accusing them of not trying hard enough.

"Our next response to How was massive inspection. We figured that by just examining everything with the finest of fine-toothed combs, we simply *couldn't* have any Quality problems, could we? But that didn't work because people just assumed that mistakes would be caught by the inspectors, so they got more careless, and more mistakes than ever were made!

"Our third answer to How was moving to a prevention mind-set. And that seemed to be working until . . . well, until this." And as he said this (or more precisely, as he said "this"), The Boss sifted his fingers through the dusty black heap of punctuation marks on the conference table.

The Boss continued: "All of those things—What, How, inspection, prevention—represented real progress. They were important and necessary parts of the solution. But I realized that if we were ever going to get to the bottom of this thing, it would be necessary for each department to understand what Theory Why meant to their own operations. That's why I had to do what I did.

That's why you were relieved of your responsibilities for Quality."

The right-hand man and left-hand man were now pretty sure that they weren't being blamed for anything. But they still didn't *really* understand what The Boss was getting at.

The Boss continued: "When we turned things back over to the operating departments, what did we discover?"

"They all knew that the answer to What was 'Quality problems,' " said the left-hand man.

"And they all had different answers to How," said the right-hand man.

"Exactly!" said The Boss. "Each manager had a perfectly reasonable, perfectly logical response to How to achieve higher Quality.

"The Manufacturing Manager saw his job to be removing every possible distraction from his workers' quest for Quality.

"The Human Resources Manager decided to design in higher levels of Quality through an improved orientation process.

"The Finance Manager decided to build in financial incentives toward achieving higher levels of Quality.

"The Engineering Manager developed some formal systems to assure higher levels of Quality.

"And the Marketing Manager saw it as her job to communicate and promote the importance of Quality far and wide.

"Now, could anyone quarrel with any of those Hows?"

Both the right-hand man and left-hand man shook their heads no, in agreement.

"Of course not!" continued The Boss. "They make sense. They're logical. Goodness, they're right out of the management bibles!"

And although the left-hand man and right-hand man still weren't certain of their destination, they had begun to enjoy the ride.

Sensing this, The Boss pressed on.

"But my theory is that they won't work—they *can't* work—unless the various How's have been developed in response to the proper Why's.

"What's more, they all *sensed* that it wouldn't work," he added, thinking back to all the twinges of his operating managers, "even though they may not have realized that they sensed it."

He continued: "If there's one thing we ought to have learned by now around here, it's that achieving higher Quality is hard, hard work. And people need to have a reason to do hard, hard work. You heard the Manufacturing Manager say it very clearly to me not 15 minutes ago: 'I resent this. You're asking us to do all this work, and you can't even tell us why!'"

The light was beginning to dawn on the right-hand man and the left-hand man.

"With us running the show," continued The Boss, "Why was 'because corporate headquarters—those guys in their ivory tower—said so.' And that won't get it done over the long haul. So I had to give responsibility back to the line people—all line people, in all departments.

"Now, Why wasn't 'because corporate headquarters said so' any more. Why was 'productivity' in the manufacturing department, and 'morale' in the human resources department, and 'profitability' in the finance department, and 'technology' in the engineering department, and 'market share' in the marketing department," said The Boss.

"And don't get me wrong. Those are all good, important things. But they're not really objectives; they're measures. It's all a matter of focus. Focusing on those things is like a student focusing on getting A's rather than on getting educated. It's focusing on the measures, on the score. And when you focus on the score, it all tends to become a game.

"And we get so wrapped up in playing that game that we lose sight of the object: to serve the customer.

"You saw the Quality projects that had been set up in each department, right?"

The right-hand man and left-hand man nodded their agreement.

"Okay," The Boss continued. "How do you suppose it would be viewed in the manufacturing department if a customer offered a suggestion to make the process work better?"

"A distraction," said the left-hand man, thinking back to his visit to the manufacturing department.

"It would hurt productivity," said the right-hand man, beginning to understand what The Boss was driving at.

"Exactly!" said The Boss. "How do you suppose customer concerns would fit into the new orientation package in the human resources department?"

"A bother," said the right-hand man.

"Customer concerns and complaints do more damage to morale than any other single thing," said the left-hand man.

"Exactly!" said The Boss. "And how much input do you suppose customers had to the new invoicing system set up by the finance department?"

"None," said the left-hand man. "It would have taken too much time to get their inputs, and time is money."

"And besides," said the right-hand man, "if the customers knew enough to send their payments to the right departments in the first place, there wouldn't have been any need for a new invoicing system!"

"Exactly!" said The Boss. "And how interested do you suppose the engineering department is in what customers think about the new product process?"

"Not interested at all," said the right-hand man. "I mean, if we didn't have to make products that could be used and understood by ordinary customers—nontechnical people—imagine how much faster we could get them out into the market!"

"Yeah," said the left-hand man, really getting into things now, "most customers wouldn't know a megabyte if it megabit 'em!"

"Exactly!" said The Boss. "And how concerned do you suppose the marketing department is with the usefulness of their new ad campaign for an individual customer?"

"Not at all," said the left-hand man. "They're too worried about the marketing of Quality to worry about the Quality of marketing."

"And besides," added the right-hand man, "individual customers aren't important. It's what they think in the aggregate—markets!—that counts."

"Exactly!" said The Boss. "And what do you make of all this?"

"We've lost focus on what's really important," said the left-hand man.

"We've neglected to answer the most basic question of all: Why?" said the right-hand man.

"Exactly!" cried The Boss, for the umpteenth time. And for the very first time, the right-hand man and the left-hand man knew *exactly* what he was saying.

And now, certain that they truly understood, The Boss could tell them what he had gradually become more and more convinced of over these past, trying months.

"Please understand, that I'm not talking about people not doing their jobs. The problems were caused because people were doing their jobs *too well*," said The Boss, paradoxically.

"I asked you two to give up your Quality responsibilities because the skill with which you did your jobs led others to take the solution to our Quality problems for granted.

"Similarly, the various department managers have done a very good job of communicating goals, putting into place programs to achieve those goals, and getting results as measured against those goals. And that is a pretty good definition of good management.

"No, throughout all of this, there really has been only one person who hasn't done the job he was being paid to do. And that person is . . . me."

The right-hand man and left-hand man started to come to The Boss's defense.

The Boss sensed their disagreement and held up a palm to ward off any objections.

"I'm not going to make any grandstand plays, or say that I haven't cared just as much or tried just as hard as the next person. But, in the final analysis, the issue is one of focus, one of answering the question

Why? And any way you look at it, that *is* my job.

"We think we've reached an exalted level of enlightenment when we say: 'Quality is *the* most important factor in achieving our business objectives.' But Quality isn't the most important factor in doing business successfully: It *is* doing business successfully.

"The problem with focusing on things like productivity or morale or profitability or technology or market share is that those things can get pretty complicated. And in the process, you can convince yourself that they're so complicated that they're not fully under your control.

"But suppose you try a much much simpler focus, a simpler notion of Quality, that helps cut through a lot of the complications:

Quality means delivering the value that your customers paid for.

I defy you to challenge that definition."

, , , . . . ? ? ? ! ! !
, , , . . . ? ? ? ! ! !
, , , . . . ? ? ? ! ! !
, , , . . . ? ? ? ! ! !

And judging from the look they saw in The Boss's eyes, the right-hand man and left-hand man were relieved to realize that they had no reason to issue such a challenge.

The Boss continued: "And I defy you to find any hiding places, any loopholes, any trap doors in that definition."

Neither the right-hand man nor the left-hand man was inclined to look.

"That's why Quality is so important to your business—because it *is* your business.

"Quality is just the Value you're delivering to your customers viewed from the inside out. Value is just the Quality you produce viewed from the outside in. It's all that your customers are buying. It's all that you have for sale.

"That, gentlemen, is what we've been struggling with for lo these many months."

And, for the first time, the right-hand man and the left-hand man truly understood Why.

Why Quality was so important . . .

Why The Boss had relieved them of their Quality responsibilities . . .

Why The Boss had let the operating managers discover the secret for themselves . . .

Why The Boss had done many of the things he had done over the past three months, things that had seemed so puzzling at the time, but that made such perfect, perfect sense now.

Both the right-hand man and the left-hand man knew Quality when they saw it, and they saw it in the masterful way The Boss had managed things over the past three months.

And at that moment they knew, down in the deepest recesses of deep, that it really would be different this time.

I t had only been a month since The Boss's last visit to the manufacturing department, but the changes were subtly dramatic.

Fork lifts still whizzed, and assembly lines still ran, and machines still whirred, and whistles still blew, and wheels still turned, and cranks still cranked, and people still scurried and scuttled and scampered.

But gone were the signs dispensing variations on a "Quality Means Productivity and Productivity's What We're Here For!" theme.

In their place was a simpler, clearly focused message: *It's your job to* produce *. . . for the* Customer!

All this made The Boss very excited, for it told him that the Manufacturing Manager understood what Theory Why was all about.

And that excitement was nothing to the excitement he felt when he, the right-hand man, the left-hand man, and the Manufacturing Manager reached the assembly/painting area that they had visited before.

For before them were the assembler and the painter, huddled together, poring over a batch of commas, talking animatedly.

"My, my, my!" said The Boss. "I'm certainly surprised to see this!"

"Yes," said the right-hand man. "They're not focusing on their work like they used to. Won't the distractions cause more defects?"

"Yes," said the left-hand man. "They're talking to each other. Won't that slow down productivity?"

The Manufacturing Manager smiled. "A month ago I would have said you were right. I would also have told them to get back to work. But then it hit me: Why are they in those jobs in the first place? Is it to crank out commas, or to deliver something of value to our customers?"

Then, gesturing toward the assembler and the painter, he added, "Let's take a closer look."

And as the foursome approached, the twosome glanced up, nodded their welcome, and continued their discussion.

"If you attach the A-47 to the C/26-B at an angle of 12 degrees, 11 minutes rather than 13 degrees, 7 minutes," said the painter to the assembler, "I will be better able to get complete paint coverage down around the joint."

"Why," said The Boss, politely interrupting, "is that important?"

"Because it will make the hook less susceptible to rusting out and falling off," answered the painter. "That's important to customers who live in humid climates."

"But won't it be much harder to assemble it at that sharper angle?" asked the right-hand man. "That looks pretty tricky to me."

"Maybe so," said the assembler. "But, you know, I could make it *really* easy on myself by not building the thing at all! You have to ask yourself: Why are we here? To meet our needs, or our customers' needs?"

"But won't all that extra care slow down productivity?" asked the left-hand man.

"Not as much as it slows down a customer when the hook rusts out and falls off in midsentence," replied the Manufacturing Manager.

The Boss, clearly thrilled, thanked the painter and the assembler for their time.

"You should be very pleased," he said to the Manufacturing Manager, as they walked toward the doors leading out of the manufacturing department.

"You don't know the half of it," said the Manufacturing Manager. "I mean, when I came down here and began talking about Why, people understood immediately! There was none of the resistance you expect when you come along with a new idea. As soon as we began focusing on Why, Quality began to go up. People were just naturally more careful, but in a more purposeful, mindful way than before."

"That's great," said The Boss.

"Yes, it is," said the Manufacturing Manager. "But the thing I didn't expect was, productivity went up, too! I thought that I was being a good manager before by eliminating distractions from the workers. Well, the idea was right, but I was operating under the wrong theory."

At this, the right-hand man and the left-hand man gave The Boss a knowing glance, and he acknowledged it in a way that was apparent to them, invisible to the Manufacturing Manager.

"It suddenly dawned on me: What better way to eliminate distractions than to see to it that all of the workers are focusing their attention on the most fundamental issue of all—the reason we're in business in the first place. What could be more productive than making sure people are thinking about how they can deliver more value to our customers?"

"Exactly," said The Boss, with a smile. "Exactly."

'm just thrilled to have you—all three of you—visiting our department again!" said the Human Resources Manager as he met The Boss, the right-hand man and the left-hand man at the entrance to the human resources department.

"Well, we're very glad to be here," said The Boss, graciously answering for all three of them.

"Shall we take a walk and see our new, reoriented orientation program?" asked the Human Resources Manager, leading the way.

"Reoriented?" asked the left-hand man.

"Why?" asked the right-hand man.

"It began after a staff meeting last month," began the Human Resources Manager. "I got to thinking. Why is morale so important? Why does it matter that we have a 'nice place' to work?"

"Because it will make us happier people, better people?" offered the left-hand man.

"Because it will make Punctuation Inc. a nicer, better company?" offered the right-hand man.

"Yes," said the Human Resources Manager, "all of those things are important—equally important. But there is one thing that is far, far more important than any of those things."

"What would that be?" asked The Boss (even though he already knew the answer).

"How happy our *customers* are!" proclaimed the Human Resources Manager.

The Boss was pleased that the Human Resources Manager had, apparently, "got" Theory Why.

"Our strategy was right," continued the Human Resources Manager. "You *do* have to design the Quality in at the beginning, and in the human resources business, that means during new-employee orientation. But, as I said, we had some reorienting, some re*focusing*, of our orientation program to do."

And just as he said this, they arrived at the door, over which at one time had hung a sign that read:

New Employee Orientation

But the word "Employee" had now been crossed out and replaced by the hand-written words: "Customer-Server."

Pointing to the sign, the Human Resources Manager said, "If it's important to design the Quality in at the beginning, and orientation is the beginning, then the beginning of orientation is the best place of all to begin.

"We want them to know why they're here from the moment they walk in the door."

The Boss nodded in admiration as they entered the orientation room. Immediately, he was struck by the change.

Gone were the slides of happy Punctuation Inc. employees.

Gone were the parades of happy Punctuation Inc. employees.

Gone were the poems written by Punctuation Inc. employees, extolling their contentment on the job.

Gone was the oh-so-nice company song.

"Welcome to your first day of serving the customers of Punctuation Inc.," began the facilitator, with a new purposefulness and sense of focus.

And it was clear from the reaction of her audience that they understood *exactly* what she was saying to them. What's more, they liked what they heard!

"She's getting positive reenforcement from her audience," whispered the Human Resources Manager to The Boss.

"So she is," said The Boss, with a nod.

So you are, thought The Boss, with a smile.

And the orientation package was a roaring success.

First there was a short talk *about* Punctuation Inc. customers.

Then there was a short film *showing* Punctuation Inc. customers.

Then there were some questions asked *of* Punctuation Inc. customers.

Finally, everyone signed up to make a visit *to* a Punctuation Inc. customer after lunch.

When it was over, The Boss turned to the Human Resources Manager and said: "You've certainly come up with a high-Quality orientation package for new employees."

"Thank you," said the Human Resources Manager. "But I think you meant 'new customer-servers.'"

"Yes, of course," said The Boss. "I guess I'm not quite as focused as you are yet. You should be very proud—and very happy."

The right-hand man and left-hand man smiled in admiration. (When it occurred to them that they were doing a lot of that lately, they smiled in admiration again.)

"Yes, I am," said the Human Resources Manager. "And do you know what the most amazing thing of all is?"

"No, what?" asked The Boss (although he knew exactly what the most amazing thing of all was).

"We decided to focus our Quality efforts on the customer rather than on morale. And yet, not only has Quality improved, morale has improved, too! I mean, just look at her!"

And as he said this, the Human Resources Manager pointed to the facilitator, who was beaming with satisfaction at the effectiveness of her orientation efforts.

"That's remarkable," said the left-hand man.

"That's amazing," said the right-hand man.

"That's excellent managing," said The Boss. "Congratulations."

The Human Resources Manager was clearly gratified.

Almost, but not quite, as gratified as The Boss.

ello, Junior!" said The Boss.

Ka-*chunkkk!*

"Hello," Junior said to The Boss, adding welcoming nods to the right-hand man, the left-hand man, and the Finance Manager.

"Our guests are here to talk about the improvements we've made to our Quality project, Junior," said the Finance Manager.

Ka-*chunkkk!*

"Why did you punch out?" asked the right-hand man.

"Aren't you going to charge back the time you spend with us?" asked the left-hand man.

"No, I'm not," said Junior. "Time spent talking about our Quality project is time spent talking about customers. And time spent talking about customers is not an expense; it's an investment. About the best investment we can make."

"There are tax advantages, too," gushed the Finance Manager with pride.

"Well, there's nothing *wrong* with profit,"

said Junior (unnecessarily) defensively. "It's just that profit ought to be viewed as the by-product of doing other things right. Not as the primary focus."

The Boss was amazed that such a change could have occurred in just one month's time.

"I'm glad to hear you talking that way," said The Boss to Junior. Then, to the Finance Manager, he added, "You said something about improvements made to your Quality project?"

"Yes," replied the Finance Manager. "We thought we were doing so well because our eraser-rental figures were dropping. We concluded from that that the cost of errors was dropping. Quality was improving, and that was, therefore, better. But then we started asking ourselves a very basic and important question: Why?"

"Eraser rentals *were* down," said Junior, picking up the thread of the argument. "Fewer mistakes *were* being made. Costs *were* down. Trouble is," concluded Junior, "we were focusing on the wrong costs."

"What do you mean?" asked the right-hand man.

"We were looking at it in terms of what it cost *us*," answered Junior.

"What's wrong with that?" asked the left-hand man.

"If all we're going to think about is *our* costs, well, then why not get out of the business altogether? I mean, that would drive *our* costs down to zero."

"But when we began asking why, we saw the light," added the Finance Manager. "We asked ourselves, 'Why are we in business at all?' And the answer we came up with was pretty basic: to deliver value to our customers."

"But what about profitability?" asked The Boss, testing.

"The more value we deliver, the more profit we'll make," replied the Finance Manager. "At least that's the way it ought to work."

"And it turns out that it *does* work that way," chimed in Junior. "The way we had set things up—asking our customers to deal with a different invoice for each product they ordered—didn't really reduce costs. It just transferred them: from us to our customers, since they had to spend time figuring out which invoice went with which order and where to send them all. And higher costs to our customers means less value for them. And ultimately, less profit for us."

"Remember that our paper clip sales had fallen off?" asked the Finance Manager.

"Yes, I do," replied The Boss.

"Well, paper clip sales had fallen off because the number of invoices we had to handle had fallen off. And the number of invoices had fallen off because sales of Punctuation Inc. products had fallen off."

"And sales of Punctuation Inc. products had fallen off because we had effectively raised their price through our 'improved Quality,'" added Junior. "We began to turn things around when we changed the focus of our Quality program, from 'minimizing costs to us' to 'maximizing value to our customers.'"

"As a result of changing your focus, what have you done differently?" asked The Boss.

"First of all," said the Finance Manager, "we redesigned our invoicing forms. To be sure we did it right this time, we went out and asked our customers what they did and didn't like about our invoices. And we got an earful."

"I can imagine," said the right-hand man and the left-hand man. "They must have resented your taking their time. Time is money, you know."

"But they didn't!" said the Finance Manager. "In fact, they were thrilled that we asked. And they gave us many excellent ideas which we incorporated into our new forms.

"So you're right: time *is* money. And all in all, our refocused Quality effort has been time very well spent indeed!"

The Boss and the Finance Manager shook hands, and as they did, the right-hand man whispered to the left-hand man, "I think there may be something to this Theory Why business."

"Exactly," whispered the left-hand man, smiling and nodding. "Exactly."

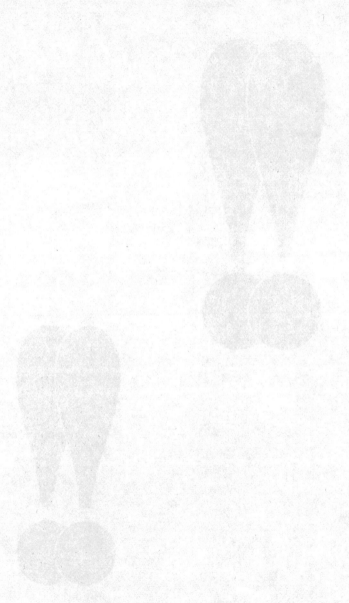

have developed a theory which addresses our Quality problems," said the Engineering Manager with her customary precision and forthrightness.

"You've developed a theory?" asked the left-hand man.

"Especially for our Quality problems?" asked the right-hand man.

"Could the Wright Brothers fly?" answered the Engineering Manager.

"What is your theory?" asked The Boss (but, of course, he already knew the answer).

"The basic premise of my theory," began the Engineering Manager, "is that you will improve the Quality of your product designs more effectively by focusing on serving customers' needs rather than on technological breakthroughs."

The Boss was impressed by the matter-of-fact way in which the Engineering Manager described such a fundamental change in her basic position.

"I'm impressed by the matter-of-fact way in which you describe such a fundamental change in your basic position," said The Boss.

"You've got to be adaptable, or you won't make it in this business," said the Engineering Manager. "I think Darwin said that first."

"So what are some of the adaptations you made?" asked the left-hand man.

"Well, for example," began the Engineering Manager. "Do you remember the digital question marks we were working on the last time you were here?"

"Yes," said The Boss.

"We were really hung up on that one," said the Engineering Manager. "We seemed to be going nowhere. Then we decided to apply my theory. We talked to some customers about the new technology. And they set us straight."

"They showed you where the problems were with your digital question marks?" asked the right-hand man.

"No," said the Engineering Manager. "They showed us that our problem *was* our digital question marks. The application was wrong. And they steered us toward a far more viable application: digital quotation marks for journalists who need 100 percent accuracy in quoting sources."

??? ??? ???

"What a great idea!" said the left-hand man and the right-hand man.

"It was completed more quickly, was of higher Quality, and it came from a customer," said the Engineering Manager, adding ironically, "who would have thought it?

"Remember the underwater punctuation marks project?"

"Yes," said The Boss. "But wasn't that an *old* project even a month ago?"

"That's one way of looking at it. But then, there's another way of looking at it," said the Engineering Manager, gesturing toward her lead engineer hard at work at the back of the lab.

The Boss walked over to the engineer.

"Hello," he said. "I see you're still working on those watertight punctuation marks."

"Well, not really," said the engineer. "A lot of the basic technology is the same. But when we showed the underwater punctuation marks to customers, they weren't impressed. Except for one guy, a lawyer. He said that he sure could use some help constructing airtight cases for his clients, and Bingo! A slight change in the gasket design and watertight becomes airtight! There's still some work to be done, but now I know the work is going into a real product, with real application."

"Very impressive," said The Boss, referring to both the airtight punctuation marks and the engineer's new, Theory Why-induced focus.

"Your theory certainly seems to have made your life simpler," said the left-hand man to the Engineering Manager.

"Oh, no," said the Engineering Manager. "It's made my life far more complicated."

"Really?" said the right-hand man. "That's too bad."

"Oh, no," said the Engineering Manager. "That's good."

The Boss could see the confusion in the faces of the right-hand man and the left-hand man. "Could you explain?" he said to the Engineering Manager.

"Was Descartes coordinated?" answered the Engineering Manager. "It turned out that there's a corollary to my theory which I quickly discovered: Engineers are just as interested in getting on to the next one after you apply my theory, but 'the next one' quickly becomes 'the last one.'"

"Oh," said the right-hand man, "that's bad."

"No," said the Engineering Manager, "that's good. What could be better than having all of our engineers wanting to spend more and more time with our customers in an effort to make our existing products—'the last ones'—better and better?"

"But that must slow things down," said the right-hand man.

"No," said the Engineering Manager. "It speeds things up. By talking to customers they're getting right to the heart of *real* issues and focusing their energies and skills more directly on solving *real* problems. Real problems, I might add, which we would have wound up having to solve eventually anyway. Anybody can get a technology to market quickly. The hard part is getting new technologies into high-Quality products that meet real customer needs faster.

"Precise application of my theory makes that possible."

"Well," said The Boss, shaking the Engineering Manager's hand, "I can see that you certainly have made real progress. You should take great satisfaction in what you've accomplished."

"I do," said the Engineering Manager. And then she added, "I hope you realize how grateful we all are for the opportunity you've given us to develop our own solutions."

"Did Galileo know what revolved around what?" responded The Boss.

And then they all laughed.

And the right-hand man and left-hand man knew that Galileo had nothing on The Boss.

o," said The Boss, after he and the right-hand man and the left-hand man had listened to the Marketing Manager describe the change in focus of her department's Quality efforts, "you're saying that marketing has a key Quality role to play in keeping the organization as a whole focused on its distinctive competency in order to satisfy the demands of a complex and dynamic marketplace?"

"Well," said the Marketing Manager with a shrug, "you could say it that way. I prefer to put it in simpler terms."

"Which are?" asked The Boss.

"We have to deliver to customers what they paid us for," said the Marketing Manager. "After all, isn't that why we exist?"

"Exactly!" said the right-hand man.

"Exactly!" said the left-hand man.

"Exactly," said The Boss. "It sounds great in theory. Have you put any of those ideas into practice yet?"

"You bet," replied the Marketing Manager. "Remember the semicolon ad campaign we showed you the last time you were here?"

The Boss, the right-hand man, and the left-hand man all nodded yes.

"Well," the Marketing Manager continued, "instead of simply trying to be clever and blow smoke at the customer, we're actually looking at this advertising/promotion effort as an opportunity to deliver even more value. Value in the form of clearer, more useful information."

And as she said this, she turned on a videotape of a recent talk between her lead marketing specialist and a customer, who were discussing the material spread out on the table in front of them: a document describing the half-price pricing stratgy for the new semicolon, the brushed-leather semicolon carrying case, and the proposed "There's nothing semi/half-baked/halfway about the quality of our semicolon!" ad campaign.

The customer seemed totally uninterested in any of it. "I suppose it's okay," he said with a shrug, "but . . . I mean . . . what does any of it mean to me?"

"Could you elaborate?" said the marketing specialist.

"First of all," the customer said, "you hit me with 'half-price.' But price isn't the only thing I think about. Tell me how much it costs, yes, but make sure you tell me what it will do for me. Then I can figure out the value I get—which, when you get right down to it, is what I'm really buying."

The marketing specialist nodded, taking careful notes.

"And these ads!" added the customer, picking up a sample layout. *"I'll* be the judge of quality, if you don't mind!"

"You said that, given the right information, you could figure out the value of the product," said the marketing specialist. "But the ad talked about quality. Can you explain the difference between the two?"

"Simple," said the customer. " 'Value' is the word I used. 'Quality' is the word you used."

"And that's the difference?" asked the marketing specialist.

"Far as I'm concerned," replied the customer.

, , ,   · · ·   ? ? ?   ! ! !
, , ,   · · ·   ? ? ?   ! ! !

, , ,   · · ·   ? ? ?   ! ! !
, , ,   · · ·   ? ? ?   ! ! !

, , ,   · · ·   ? ? ?   ! ! !
, , ,   · · ·   ? ? ?   ! ! !

(The Boss looked at his three co-workers and slowly nodded. They returned his nod.)

Back on the videotape, the marketing specialist pointed to the brushed-leather carrying case and said to the customer: "I suppose, then, that you wouldn't find that terribly interesting. It was just a little gimmick we were going to use to promote the Quality of our semicolons."

The customer picked up the carrying case. "This reminds me of the camping trips I used to go on when I was a boy. Makes me think of the leather case that I carried my trusty hunting knife in."

The marketing specialist was only half listening. "Funny you should mention a knife," he said, rolling a semicolon around distractedly in his fingers. "One of our people said that these semicolons are the Swiss Army knives of punctuation."

"What do you mean?" asked the customer.

"Well," said the marketing specialist, "in just one piece of punctuation, you've got a semicolon"—he detached the semicolon's dot from its hook and held them up, one in each hand—"a period, and a comma."

"I never thought of it that way," said the customer, his eyes brightening.

The marketing specialist began to warm to the task. "Take two semicolons, and you've got two of each of these"—he detached the dots and hooks of two semicolons and rearranged them—"or a colon and a set of punctuation marks, closed or open, your choice."

"That's great!" exulted the customer. "I've been looking for something like that for a long, long time!"

"You have?" asked the marketing specialist.

"Yes," said the customer. "I still do a lot of hunting. And all of that traipsing through the woods can get pretty tiring. So at night, while we're gathered around the campfire, I'm not so much one for conversation as I used to be. I'd like to be, but I just don't have the energy to carry all of those extra punctuation marks with me, so I don't talk as much. But with these"—he held up a Punctuation Inc. semicolon admiringly—"why I'd pay twice as much for these!"

The Marketing Manager switched off the tape. "As I was saying," she said, "there is a lot to be gained by viewing Quality from the customer's point of view."

Which, the right-hand man and the left-hand man suddenly realized, is exactly what The Boss had done over these past three months: looked at Quality from the point of view of one very important set of *his* customers—the Manufacturing Manager, and the Human Resources Manager, and the Finance Manager, and the Engineering Manager, and the Marketing Manager.

They slowly shook their heads in admiration.

"Chalk the Jeep!" whispered the right-hand man to the left-hand man.

"Exactly," whispered the left-hand man to the right-hand man. "Exactly!"

Epilogue

The Boss had found his staff meetings to be ever so much more productive, effective, and, yes, enjoyable over the past six months. Or ever since the basic insight of Theory Why had been simultaneously discovered by everyone, it seemed, at Punctuation Inc.

For one thing, Theory Why had made it easier to focus in on the meeting's agenda, providing as it did a standard framework that could be applied each and every week:

Discussion and resolution of customer problems

Discussion and resolution of customer suggestions

Profile and discussion of new customers

Updates and discussion of old customers

Visits by customers

Any other business (which must, in
one way or another, be directly and
explicitly connected to the need to
"deliver value to our customers")

How had we managed to let the business get so complicated? he thought, as he
looked around the room and saw the people who had helped him steer Punctuation
Inc. through its Quality problems.

Who would have thought, his thoughts
went on, that by merely focusing our attention on the customer, we could, in one fell
swoop:

Improve Quality
Improve productivity
Improve morale
Improve profitability
Get new technologies to market
more quickly, and
Gain market share.

What could be more simple? he
thought, and then, as the memory of the
months and months of hard work and frustration came back to him, he also thought, or
more difficult?

He started when he realized that everyone was staring expectantly at him. But
he knew them well enough, and they knew
him well enough, that he could afford to be
totally honest.

"I'm sorry," he said, "but my mind wandered. Would you please bring me back to earth?"

The right-hand man spoke first. "It seems that the Quality efforts of Punctuation Inc. have not gone unnoticed. In fact, they have been extremely well noticed."

The Boss was very interested in what the right-hand man was saying. But he was even more interested in the broad smiles adorning the faces of the right-hand man, the left-hand man, the Manufacturing Manager, the Human Resources Manager, the Finance Manager, the Engineering Manager, and the Marketing Manager, since they signaled to him a very clear message: Everyone else knew something that he didn't know.

"In fact," continued the left-hand man, pulling a piece of paper from a folder in front of him and the right-hand man, "not only have they been noticed, they have been officially recognized."

The Boss was beginning to get the gist of what was unfolding, and he wasn't sure that it was all to his liking.

"Whereas," the left-hand man and the right-hand man began, reading in unison from the piece of paper, "Punctuation Inc. has demonstrated unique and purposeful focus in striving for improved Quality . . .

"And whereas," they continued, "the efforts of Punctuation Inc. have served as an inspiration to all organizations engaged in a similar struggle for the attainment of ever higher levels of Quality . . .

"And whereas said focus and striving and struggle are all embodied in the persona of one man, to wit The Boss . . .

"We, the Worldwide Business Association, do hereby and solemnly proclaim said The Boss as the Quality Man of the Year!"

At that The Boss's staff rose and applauded and applauded and then continued to applaud some more.

The Boss was moved—by the honor, but even more so by the demonstration of respect and affection from the people who had made this honor possible.

He gestured for them to stop and—three such gestures later—they complied.

He began to speak, but the words didn't come out easily. "Boy," he said, clearing his throat, "it feels like I've swallowed a whole package of Industrial Grade Ellipses!"

They all laughed, sympathetically giving him time to compose himself.

Then he continued: "I am very moved to have been given this award and will be very honored to accept it—under one condition."

At this the others were startled. They knew that The Boss had been named for the award and they were delighted for him. But they never dreamed that he would do anything but accept it with open arms. After all, he certainly deserved it!

The Boss continued: "The citation calls

me the Quality Man of the Year. And that implies that it was I, alone, who accomplished what we've accomplished.

"But it wasn't just me. It was all of us in this room, as well as all the people who work in all jobs for Punctuation Inc.

"And it was all of our customers, who—even though we were too smart to listen for a long, long time—were willing and able to tell us all that we needed to know about our Quality problems.

"They most certainly did know it when they saw it, and it took our eyes the longest time to focus on the 'it' that they so clearly saw. But eventually we did. And it was the result of a lot of caring, and dedication, and hard work—most especially on the part of the people in this room.

"So . . . I will accept this award, but only if you will all accept it jointly with me. Is that agreed to?"

Everyone's first inclination was to go along with The Boss, because, after all, he was The Boss, and that carried a high degree of "going-along-with" with it.

But then, all at once, an infectious grin started to spread around the table. It wasn't at all clear who had started to grin first. But, very quickly, the only one not grinning was The Boss.

"Well," he said, a little uncomfortably, "is it?"

And, believe it or not, this is how they answered:

"No," said the left-hand man, grinning.

"No," said the right-hand man, grinning.

"No," said the Manufacturing Manager, and the Human Resources Manager, and the Finance Manager, and the Engineering Manager, and the Marketing Manager—all at the same time, grinning.

The Boss was taken aback. "You mean you won't accept the award with me?" he asked.

"That's right," said the left-hand man.

"That's right," said the right-hand man.

"That's right," said the Manufacturing Manager, and the Human Resources Manager, and the Finance Manager, and the Engineering Manager, and the Marketing Manager—all at the same time, all still grinning.

"But," asked The Boss in despair, "Why?"

"Exactly!"

And, at that exact instant, The Boss knew, as certainly as he had ever known anything before, that Punctuation Inc.'s Quality problems were behind them.

And that Quality opportunities lay ahead.